SPORTS ALL-ST★RS

BREANNA STEWART

Jon M. Fishman

Lerner Publications ◆ Minneapolis

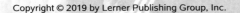

Lerner Publications Company
A division of Lerner Publishing Group, Inc.
241 First Avenue North
Minneapolis, MN 55401 USA

For reading levels and more information, look up this title at www.lernerbooks.com.

Main body text set in Albany Std 15/22. Typeface provided by Agfa.

Library of Congress Cataloging-in-Publication Data

Names: Fishman, Jon M., author.
Title: Breanna Stewart / Jon M. Fishman.
Description: Minneapolis : Lerner Publications, [2019] | Series: Sports all-stars | Includes bibliographical references and index. | Audience: Grade 4 to 6.
Identifiers: LCCN 2018006140 (print) | LCCN 2018019794 (ebook) | ISBN 9781541524668 (eb pdf) | ISBN 9781541524583 (lb : alk. paper) | ISBN 9781541528048 (pb : alk. paper)
Subjects: LCSH: Stewart, Breanna, 1994—–Juvenile literature. | Women basketball players—United States—Biography—Juvenile literature. | Basketball players—United States—Biography.
Classification: LCC GV884.S74 (ebook) | LCC GV884.S74 F57 2019 (print) | DDC 796.323092 [B] —dc23

LC record available at https://lccn.loc.gov/2018006140

Manufactured in the United States of America
1-44534-34784-5/4/2018

CONTENTS

STORMY SKY

Breanna Stewart jumps for the tip-off against the Chicago Sky.

Seattle Storm forward Breanna Stewart bent her knees. She raised the basketball above her head and jumped, releasing the ball. *Swish!* It sailed through the net for two points.

The score brought Seattle to within three points of the Chicago Sky, 71–68. It was September 3, the final game of the 2017 regular season for the Storm. They had lost the previous three games in a row. This was the last chance to end their losing streak before the playoffs began.

Chicago led by six points with about five minutes left in the game. Suddenly, Jewell Loyd threw a pass to Stewart near the basket.

Stewart sank a **layup**.

Every time Seattle closed the gap in the score, Chicago pulled ahead again. But Stewart kept fighting. She was full of energy and confidence at both ends of the court.

Stewart keeps the ball away from a Sky player.

Stewart made a long shot with less than two minutes on the game clock. It finally gave Seattle the lead, 81–80. But Chicago had plenty of time to take the lead back.

The Storm played tough defense. Chicago's Cappie Pondexter jumped to take a shot. Stewart stretched her long arm and swatted the ball away from the basket.

Stewart sank two **free throws** in the final seconds to secure the win for Seattle, 85–80. She led all players in the game with 29 points. The Storm celebrated the end of their losing streak, but they couldn't start a winning streak. They lost a few days later in the playoffs.

The loss marked the end of Stewart's second year in the Women's National Basketball Association (WNBA). Losing in the playoffs hurt, but she had blossomed into a superstar during the season. The Storm had a bright future.

Stewart made almost 80 percent of her free throws in 2017.

GAME PLAYER

Breanna scores for the Cicero-North Syracuse Northstars in the 2012 Spalding Hoopball Classic.

Breanna Stewart was born on August 27, 1994, near Syracuse, New York. She grew up in Cicero, a suburb of Syracuse.

Breanna was a tall, active girl. She preferred playing games to playing with toys. She liked board games such as Candy Land. She also liked to play sports.

Softball was the first sport Breanna played, but she didn't stay with it. Then she tried basketball. She began playing when she was eight years old. She loved to help her team win.

Breanna drives the ball down the court during a high school game.

Bob Zywicki coached a youth basketball team in Syracuse. Breanna joined the team when she was ten years old. Coach Zywicki knew she didn't have the same skills as other players on the team.

Breanna defends the hoop in a high school championship game.

He later admitted that he asked her to join because she was tall. Breanna had a lot to learn about basketball. "I knew right away some of the kids on the team were much more skilled than I was," she said. "They'd all played longer than I had."

Breanna worked hard to improve. She would **dribble** around the block where she

Breanna was usually the tallest player on her youth basketball teams. She stood 6 feet (1.8 m) tall when she was in sixth grade. She reached 6 feet 4 inches (1.9 m) by the time she finished high school.

lived four times every day. She dribbled with both hands and tried spins and other moves. Later, she noticed that she was the only girl on her team who couldn't dribble between her legs. It was winter and too cold to go around the block, so Breanna practiced the move in her basement until she mastered it.

Her hard work showed on the court. Breanna began playing for the Cicero-North Syracuse High School **varsity** team when she was in eighth grade. In five seasons, she scored more than 2,300 points and helped the team win two state championships.

Breanna's height and talent caught the attention of colleges around the country.

Breanna sinks a layup!

One school stood out from the rest. The University of Connecticut (UCONN) has a history of basketball success. By 2010, Coach Geno Auriemma had led the UCONN Huskies to seven national championships. Stewart wanted to be part of it. She joined UCONN in 2013.

Left to right: Stewart celebrates with UCONN coach Geno Auriemma and teammates Morgan Tuck and Kia Nurse after winning the 2016 college basketball championship.

Stewart's hard work off the court helps her play well on the court.

Stewart doesn't dribble around her block or practice in her basement anymore. Yet her desire to get better is stronger than ever. She has worked hard to improve at every stage of her career.

At UCONN, Stewart and her teammates played more than 30 games in a season. They spent hours practicing for each game. They also lifted weights in the gym each week. As a WNBA superstar, Stewart works even harder than she did in college. "It's on me to really take my game to the next level and see how far I can go," she said.

Tough workouts helped keep Stewart at the top of her game while playing for UCONN.

Stewart practices shooting during pregame warm-ups.

Seattle Storm practices are fast-paced and exciting. Players dribble to the basket and then pass to a teammate at the last second. They run to a spot on the court, catch the ball, and pass it away quickly. They shoot, dribble, and jump. As the players work, head coach Dan Hughes shouts instructions and cheers them on.

Stewart's dribbling ability sets her apart from many other players. She continues to sharpen this skill in the WNBA. For example, she may place a plastic ring on the gym floor. Stewart dribbles in and out of the ring quickly. Then she does the same drill while dribbling two balls at once!

In another drill, Stewart sets a rope on the floor. Then she dribbles back and forth across the rope. Or she may set up cones or barrels on the court. Stewart dribbles around the barrels. Then she drives to the basket or takes a long shot.

Healthful foods give Stewart energy. But she also enjoys snack foods from time to time. Skittles and cookies are favorites of hers. She also likes homemade treats, such as her grandmother's clam chowder.

Stewart and her teammates spend time in the weight room too. Heavy weights strengthen their arms and legs. They use gear such as **medicine balls** to strengthen core muscles. These muscles in the stomach and back help Stewart keep her balance on the court.

Workouts and practices burn lots of **calories**. Some WNBA players lose weight as the season goes on. To refuel her body, Stewart eats special high-calorie bars. The bars keep her at a healthful weight and give her the energy she needs on the court.

Working out and eating well give Stewart the power to sink her shots.

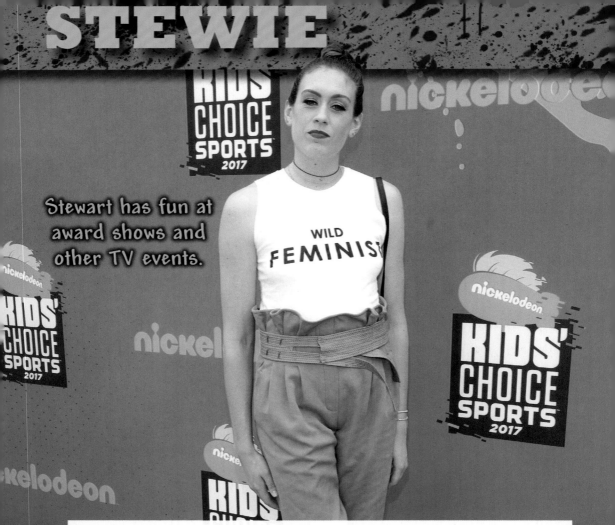

Stewart has fun at award shows and other TV events.

Some Breanna Stewart fans have watched her play for years. Yet there's always more to learn about the Seattle Storm superstar. For example, did you know that she has two pet dogs? Or that she knows how to juggle?

Friends and teammates sometimes call her Stewie. Her favorite musician is Beyoncé, and she loves the Harry Potter series. If she wasn't a sports star, she says she might be a chef.

Basketball fans are glad that Stewart chose sports. She's becoming more popular all the time. You can see her in TV commercials for the WNBA.

Stewart accepted the Best Female Athlete award during the 2016 ESPYs.

She has used her growing fame to send a message about the equal treatment of women in sports. In 2016, Stewart won an **ESPY** for Best Female Athlete. In her speech at the awards show, she wondered why the WNBA didn't receive the same attention that men's basketball received. "This has to change," she said. "Together, let's be better."

Stewart had some wacky fun at another awards show the next year. She appeared at the 2017 Nickelodeon Kids' Choice Sports Awards show. She played a game similar to musical chairs. Stewart beat Olympic skier Lindsey Vonn and other famous people to win the game!

Left to right: World Cup skier Lindsey Vonn, Breanna Stewart, and TV personality Nick Cannon participated in the Beats N Seats competition during the 2017 Nickelodeon Kids' Choice Sports Awards.

Jersey Frenzy

How do you tell which players in a league are most popular with fans? One way is by jersey sales. When fans fall in love with

a player, they often buy a **replica** of that player's jersey. In 2017, Stewart's replica jersey was second in sales in the **WNBA** (the Washington Mystics' Elena Delle Donne was first).

That means you'll see lots of fans wearing Stewart jerseys when you go to a Storm game. You may also see people wearing **KD8 NIKEiD** shoes. These sneakers in Seattle Storm colors were designed by Nike especially to honor Stewart.

Stewart's green jersey and the Nikes designed for her (*both pictured here*) are popular among Seattle Storm fans.

WORLD TRAVELER

Stewart shoots for the UCONN Huskies in a 2013 championship game.

Is Stewart the best player in women's college basketball history? Some fans think so. Her record of success at UCONN is incredible.

As a freshman in 2012–2013, Stewart had the second-best scoring average on the team.

Stewart takes a shot against the Notre Dame Fighting Irish during the 2015 NCAA women's basketball championship.

She helped the Huskies win the **NCAA** women's basketball championship. Stewart led the team in scoring average in 2013–2014. And for the second year in a row, the Huskies became national champions.

UCONN won national titles in 2014–2015 and 2015–2016 with Stewart leading the way. That made it four championships in a row, something no school had done before. In 2016, Stewart won the women's college basketball Player of the Year award for the third straight time.

Stewart and WNBA president Lisa Borders posed with a Seattle Storm jersey after Stewart was chosen first in the 2016 WNBA draft.

Left to right: US women's basketball players Brittney Griner, Elena Delle Donne, and Stewart celebrate with their gold medals at the 2016 Olympic Games.

The WNBA held the 2016 **draft** on April 14. No one was surprised when the Storm chose Stewart with the first overall pick. But she had something else to do before joining the WNBA. Geno Auriemma coached the US women's team at the 2016 Olympic Games in Rio de Janeiro, Brazil. He wanted Stewart on the team. On August 20, they won the gold medal.

Soon after helping Team USA win gold in Brazil, Stewart flew to China. She played basketball for Shanghai Baoshan Dahua of the Women's Chinese Basketball Association. She played for the team for three months before returning to the United States.

Stewart averaged almost 20 points per game with the Storm in 2016. She won the WNBA Rookie of the Year award. She played even better in 2017, but the team lost in the playoffs to the Phoenix Mercury. Stewart knows what it takes to win. She and her teammates must always try to improve and reach for the next level. "If that happens," she says, "who knows how good we'll be?"

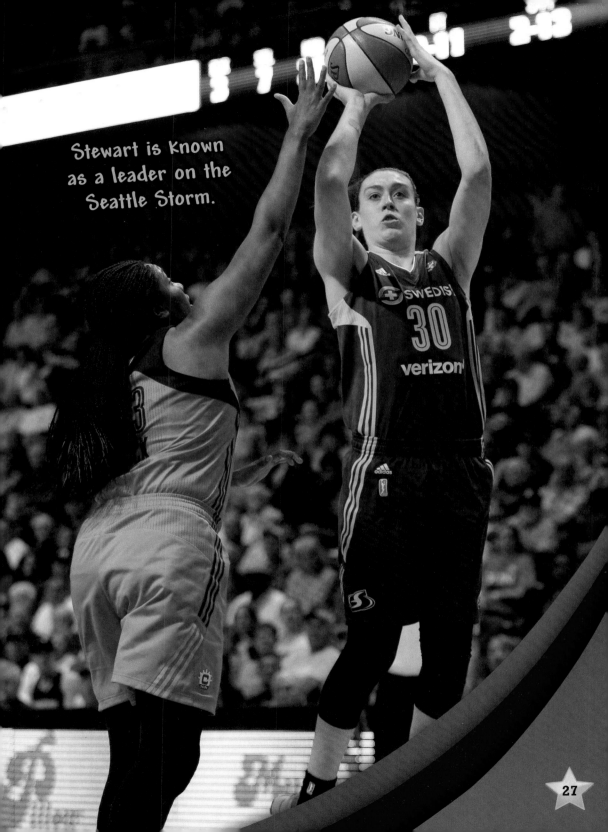

Stewart is known as a leader on the Seattle Storm.

All-Star Stats

Breanna Stewart can do it all on a basketball court. She plays tough defense and helps her teammates. She can run and jump with the best players in the world. Yet of all the things she does, scoring may be her best skill. Here's how her scoring ranks against some of the WNBA's all-time best players:

Most Points Scored per Game in WNBA History

Player	Points per Game
Cynthia Cooper	21
Elena Delle Donne	20.4
Diana Taurasi	19.8
Angel McCoughtry	19.5
Breanna Stewart	19.1
Lauren Jackson	18.9
Maya Moore	18.4
Tina Charles	18.1
Candace Parker	17.4
Lisa Leslie	17.3

Source Notes

10 John Altavilla, "Breanna Stewart: Tall on Talent, Short on Ego," *Hartford Courant*, November 11, 2014, http://www.courant.com/sports/uconn-womens-basketball/hc-ss-breanna-stewart-uconn-women-20141111-story.html.

14 "All Access: Breanna Stewart Workout," YouTube video, 1:28, posted by WNBA, April 30, 2017, https://www.youtube.com/watch?v=VhptbgD5wEo.

19 Jayda Evans, "Storm Rookie Breanna Stewart Wins ESPY, Demands Equality for Pro Female Athletes," *Seattle Times*, last modified July 14, 2016, https://www.seattletimes.com/sports/storm/storm-rookie-breanna-stewart-wins-espy-demands-equality-for-pro-female-athletes.

26 Matthew Roberson, "2017 Seattle Storm Season Recap," WNBA, September 13, 2017, http://storm.wnba.com/news/2017-seattle-storm-season-recap.

calories: units of energy in food

draft: an event in which teams take turns choosing new players

dribble: move with short bounces of the ball

ESPY: an award. ESPY stands for "Excellence in Sports Performance Yearly."

forward: a player who usually plays near the basket

free throws: unguarded shots from the free-throw line

layup: a shot taken with one hand near the basket

medicine balls: heavy balls used to strengthen muscles

NCAA: National Collegiate Athletic Association

replica: a copy

varsity: the top team at a school

Braun, Eric. *Lindsey Vonn*. Minneapolis: Lerner Publications, 2017.

Breanna Stewart
http://www.wnba.com/player/breanna-stewart

Buckley, James, Jr. *Scholastic Year in Sports 2017*. New York: Scholastic, 2017.

Jr. NBA
https://jr.nba.com

Savage, Jeff. *Basketball Super Stats*. Minneapolis: Lerner Publications, 2018.

WNBA
http://www.wnba.com

Index

Photo Acknowledgments

Image credits: iStock.com/63151 (gold and silver stars); Leon Bennett/Getty Images, p. 2; Gary Dineen/NBAE/Getty Images, pp. 4–5, 6, 7; AP Photo/Bill Shettle/Cal Sport Media, pp. 8, 11; AP Photo/Hans Pennink, pp. 9, 10; Joe Robbins/Getty Images, p. 12; Andy Lyons/Getty Images, pp. 13, 17; Michael Hickey/Getty Images, p. 14; Williams Paul/Icon Sportswire/Getty Images, pp. 15, 27; Neilson Barnard/Getty Images, p. 18; Kevin Winter/Getty Images, p. 19; Kevin Mazur/KCASports2017/WireImage/Getty Images, p. 20; Jeffrey Brown/Icon Sportswire/Newscom, p. 21; Jamie Schwaberow/NCAA Photos/Getty Images, p. 22; Mike Carlson/Getty Images, p. 23; AP Photo/Cloe Poisson/Hartford Courant, p. 24; Tom Pennington/Getty Images, p. 25.

Cover: Leon Bennett/Getty Images; iStock.com/neyro2008.